Tortois

including turtles
and terrapins.

David Robinson

John Bartholomew & Son Limited
Edinburgh and London

First published in Great Britain 1976 *by*
JOHN BARTHOLOMEW & SON LIMITED
12 Duncan Street, Edinburgh EH9 1TA
And at 216 High Street, Bromley BR1 1PW

ISBN 0 7028 1003 7

1st edition

Designed and illustrated by Allard Design Group Limited
Printed in Great Britain by W. S. Cowell Limited, Ipswich, Suffolk

Contents

Acknowledgents

Almost all books of this nature are written with the help of one authority or another, and this book is no exception. My sincere thanks go to Keith Smith, to Mr. and Mrs. Petrie of Southport Zoo, to Belle Vue Zoological Gardens and Mr. Bennet, head reptile keeper there.

Thanks are also due to the Editor of the *International Zoo Yearbook* for providing permission to use the article on breeding giant tortoises at Honolulu Zoo. I am grateful also to Eileen, my typist, for her time and patience.

Last but not least my sincere appreciation to my wife, Pauline, for her help and understanding.

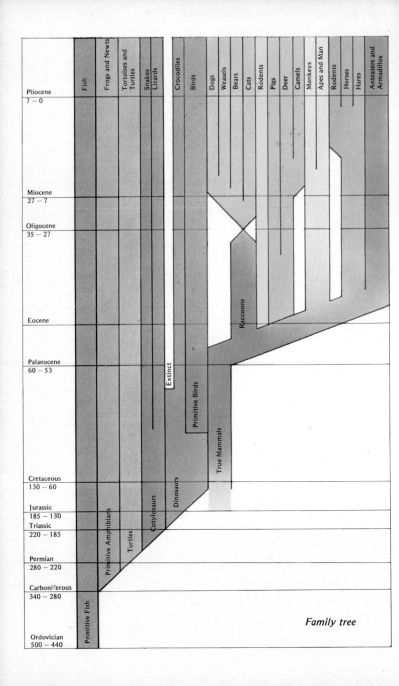

Family tree

Introduction

Tortoises are sold in pet shops the world over, but very few people stop to consider the question: just what is a tortoise, and where does it come from? The tortoises and their close relatives, the turtles, belong to the reptile family, which includes snakes, lizards, frogs and crocodiles. They are both land and water-living animals although some, such as the tortoise, prefer to spend the whole of their lives on land. The tortoise is placed well down in the family tree of these creatures, which is to say that they were among the first living animals.

The correct zoological terms to cover these creatures are as follows: Class – Reptilia, subclass – Anapsida, order – Chelonia. The Chelonia order of reptiles are all closely linked by the fact that their bodies are encased in a hard shell. The tortoise has been described by many people as a 'living fossil' and in many respects this is very true. The early prehistoric tortoise did not possess the shell as we know it today, but was covered by a series of thick scaly plates. The head, tail, and limbs of the prehistoric tortoise did not retract into the shell and therefore had to be protected in some way; it was the plates, extending some way over these exposed parts, that afforded this protection. Fossils of these creatures have been found in almost every part of the world; the largest specimen of fossilized tortoise was found in the Punjab of India by Hugh Falconer in 1835. This tortoise had a shell which measured 8 ft. in length: this would make it even larger than the Giant Galapagos Tortoise which one can see in most zoos today. There were smaller specimens roaming the earth at this time, but unfortunately for them they did not escape the attentions of primitive man for very long. Being slow and easy to capture they were used as food and the bones used to make tools and weapons. As the tortoise evolved, its armoured plates gradually grew larger and covered the whole of the creature's body to form the first type of shell.

In Biblical times tortoises were to be found all over the Mediterranean including Egypt, Syria, Israel, and Greece. Pictures have been found portraying tortoises as household pets, and sculptors and artists of this period also decorated vases, wall murals, and even tombs with the tortoise image. Musical instruments were made from the tortoise's shell, which was cleaned out and mounted on a harp-like frame in order to amplify the sound.

The tortoise is well known for its extreme longevity and ages of up to 150 years have been placed on record. Unfortunately the greater part of these records are unverifiable, although there appears to be an authentic record of a tortoise that belonged to Archbishop Laud; this tortoise lived in the gardens of Lambeth Palace and was 120 years old when it was accidentally killed by a gardener in 1753. During the days of sailing ships, tortoises were a good supply of fresh meat for the crews of the ships that visited the Galapagos Islands: the Giant Tortoises of these islands pro-

In Biblical times tortoises were found all over the Mediterranean coast, including Egypt, Syria, and Greece.

vided the sailors with enough meat to last for several months. They were rounded up in their hundreds and packed into the holds of the ship; in this way they were kept alive and killed and eaten when they were needed. The flesh was roasted and by all accounts tasted not unlike mutton. These Giant Tortoises are now protected and bred on special farms in order to preserve the species.

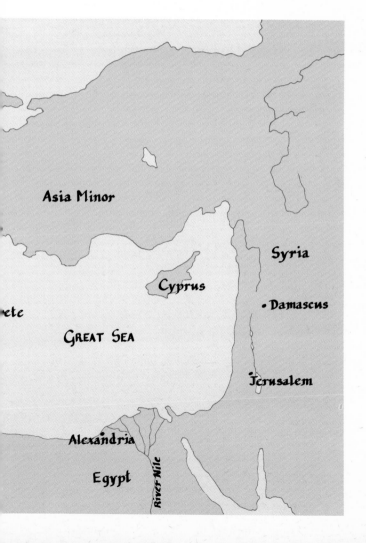

The anatomy of a tortoise

The shell

The shell of the tortoise is made up of two main parts: the upper shell, or carapace, and the lower shell, or plastron. These two shells are joined by bridges, which are located between the fore and hind limbs on both sides of the body. The shell itself is made of thick bony plates on the inside, and outer, horny plates called laminae. The laminae is produced by the growth of living cells in much the same way as most other reptiles' scales. Each set of the plates has a name and those running the full length of the back along the top are known as vertebrae. Next to these are larger plates running parallel to the vertebrae on both sides; these are costals. There is then a single plate at the head which is termed the nuchae and another plate at the tail which is the supracaudal. Around the edge of the shell the plates form a fringe and these are known as the marginal plates. These horny plates of the shell increase in size as the tortoise grows. The lower part of the shell or plastron is made up of six main plates, these are the abdominal in the middle, the pectoral at the head side of the abdominal, and the femoral on the other side, nearest the tail. There is then the humeral, which is next to the pectoral on the head side, and the anal, which is the tail section. The last one is the integular, which is positioned right at the head and is the smallest of the six plastron plates. All these plates differ in some way according to the species, and there are a variety of colours, the most common being a pale yellow darkening to orange and brown. These colours are usually combined with black markings of differing shapes and sizes. The colour and pattern of the shell contribute to the stone-like appearance and help to camouflage the tortoise in the country of its origin. The shell of the tortoise appears to stop growing when the animal hibernates each year and produces a dark ring, which has been compared by some people to the annual rings that can be seen on the cross-section of a felled tree.

The idea that one can tell the age of a tortoise by counting these rings is largely fallacious; the rings can also be caused by illness, which results in a check in the growth of the tortoise and therefore the formation of an extra ring. A common ailment of the pet tortoise is a condition known as soft shell; this is caused by a diet which is deficient in calcium and vitamin D. The whole or part of the tortoise's shell becomes soft to the touch and does not provide the protection for which it was intended. Fresh green food and plenty

Upper shell = carapace

(plates)

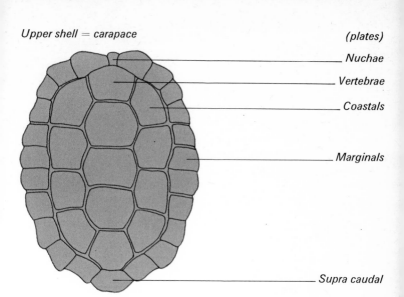

— Nuchae

— Vertebrae

— Coastals

— Marginals

— Supra caudal

Lower shell = plastron

(plates)

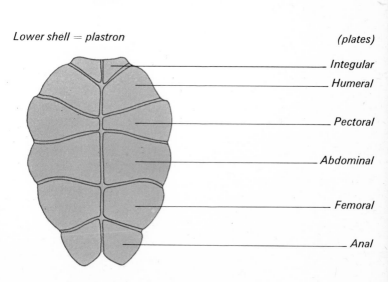

— Integular

— Humeral

— Pectoral

— Abdominal

— Femoral

— Anal

of variety in the diet will usually put things right, although the hardening process is slow. Although invaluable as a protective shield, the shell of the tortoise has one or two disadvantages. It is heavy and awkward to carry around and tends to restrict the creature's breathing. In order to breathe air the tortoise has developed a technique found in no other animal. The muscles of the stomach are divided into two parts; the first part opens the body cavity to allow the lungs to fill with air; the second part of the stomach muscles push the viscera against the lungs in order to inflate them and so expel the taken-in air. This action can be seen when a tortoise is suddenly frightened: as the limbs and head are retracted the air is expelled from the lungs and will be heard in the form of a hiss from the tortoise's nostrils. As the animal relaxes and extends its legs the process is reversed and air is taken in.

The skin

The tough leathery skin of the tortoise provides the same kind of protection as the shell, and, to allow for the movement of the limbs, has creases or folds. The skin has scales not unlike those found on most other reptiles. The scales on the tortoise's legs are larger and tougher than those found on the rest of the exposed parts, and they overlap each other to afford the protection needed for these vital limbs. Each foot carries thick stubby nails and the number of these nails also differs according to the particular species in question. In the case of the Mediterranean Tortoise, whose shell was described in the last paragraph, there are five nails on the fore foot and four nails on the hind foot. These nails are a great asset to the tortoise; they are used as tools for shredding food as well as for digging into the ground in order to escape the hot midday sun. Being a cumbersome creature, one would not imagine the tortoise to be much of a climber, but this is where the nails become useful. These nails are dug into crevices in the rock and the whole body is pulled and pushed along; progress is slow but one can be sure that the tortoise will get there in the end. Accidents do happen, of course, and if the tortoise should topple over and land on its back the nails once more come into action. The tortoise will reach over its head with a foreleg and dig the nails into the ground; the leg is then used as a lever to push the body over. The skin covering the neck and head is not quite so tough, the reason being that the head has to be retracted straight back into the shell, and in order to do this the skin has to fold. The neck is loosely skinned to allow for folding, whereas the head is hard and bony, and also covered

12

with thick scales. One of the most appealing features of the tortoise is the eyes which are solid black in colour (in most species), small, and beady. A healthy tortoise has amazingly good eyesight but as with most creatures its eyesight deteriorates with age, and some really old tortoises are unable to feed properly, often completely missing their mouths with the food. The tortoises and its chelonian relatives have no teeth, but the edges of their mouths have horny ridges, able to deal with almost any kind of food.

From one extreme to the other we now come to the tail; this is also protected by the same type of scaly skin as the head and limbs. One of the most reliable ways of sexing tortoises is by comparing the length of tail of two animals. In the female the tail is usually shorter and fatter than that of the male. Also, in the male tortoise the penis is mounted at the base of the tail, where it is fully protected.

The most reliable way to sex a tortoise is by comparing the tails. That of the female being shorter and fatter.

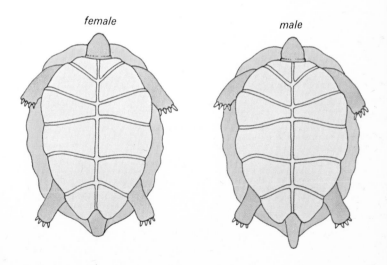

female

male

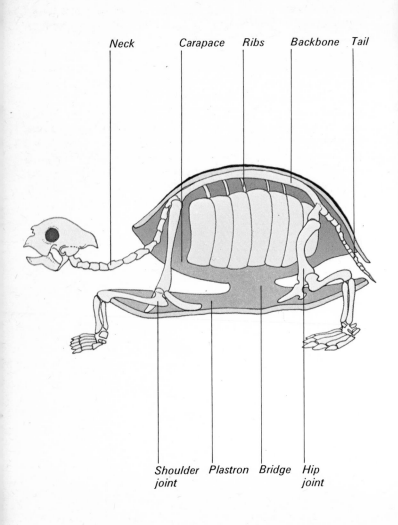

Neck   Carapace   Ribs   Backbone   Tail

Shoulder joint   Plastron   Bridge   Hip joint

Tortoise skeleton

The skeleton

When describing the skeleton of a tortoise, it would not be wrong to describe the animal as being made inside out! The shell represents the tortoise's equivalent of ribs; but while most living things have the joints of the shoulder and hips outside the rib cage, the tortoise has his inside. The ribs are almost nonexistent, as they have with time become part of the carapace. This is also true of the spine; instead of being supple and easy to bend it has become fixed and shortened. The neck and tail bones are the only freely moving parts of the spine. There are in fact some bones usually found in the reptile family that are completely absent in the tortoise; these are the breast bone, collarbone, and interclavicle. These bones are absent because the tortoise has no use for them, the shell being a kind of universal substitute. However, the shoulder blades and hip bones are quite enlarged in proportion to the size of the body as these bones are the prime source of locomotion.

Food and feeding

When a tortoise is acquired it is often true that little or no thought is given to the most vital question of what to feed, when, and where.

Unhappily, a large percentage of pet tortoises are left in the yard or garden to fend for themselves, and although perhaps not often realized, this is cruel in the extreme. Feeding is not simply a matter of throwing down a handful of lettuce leaves in the hope that the tortoise will find them, it is vital to the health, well-being, and happiness of the animal in its captive state. Tropical species of tortoise cannot hope to survive for very long if the right kind of food is not offered. In the wild state the tortoise is a great wanderer and we can therefore assume that it does not eat the same food all the time. The major part of its diet will consist of about 80 per cent vegetable matter including leaves, young shoots, and roots. The other 20 per cent will consist of fibre or animal matter such as worms, insects, and grubs. As the tortoise will eat both vegetable and animal matter it is zoologically classified as omnivorous. It is important when feeding captive tortoises to vary the diet as much as possible. This may be slightly more difficult in the winter months when certain foodstuffs are in short supply. In the summer it is of course very easy to provide fresh greenfood as well as fruit and vegetables. Tortoises, like humans, have their likes and dislikes, and it usually becomes evident within a few weeks just what a tortoise will and will not eat. Most kinds of fruit, such as melon, tomatoes, grapes, and peach, can be offered. Apples, pears, and bananas will be taken but they must be ripe and soft. Care must be taken with such fruits as they can easily be overripe and go sour; and sour fruit will cause gastric upset and could even lead to death in extreme cases. For this reason it is advisable that these foods be kept in the shade on a hot day and that anything the tortoise does not eat is removed immediately and thrown away. The staple diet will be made up mostly of vegetable matter: and here there is no substitute for young fresh lettuce. In addition, carrots, cabbage, or most kinds of non-poisonous wild weeds can be given. It is important to wash thoroughly all food offered to the tortoise; although most pesticides and crop sprays are safe and harmless to wild life, there are still one or two that can and will kill any animal that eats the infected plant. The best way to wash food for a tortoise is to hold it under a tap of cold water until all traces of dirt are completely washed away. Then the food should be hung

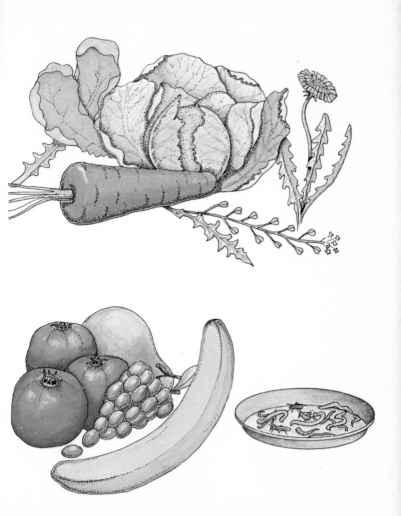

Vegetables and edible wild flowers, together
with fruit and insects, help to make up a good diet
for a tortoise.
Care should be taken to ensure all foods are
washed and dried thoroughly.

up to dry away from direct sunlight. Many of the fruit-eating tortoises will usually eat vegetables and the reverse can also be said of the vegetable-eating species. If the tortoise can be encouraged to eat both these kinds of foodstuffs then a great saving can be made in winter when some foods cannot be bought. Seasonal changes will sometimes cause a tortoise to refuse the food it has usually taken, and it will readily consume something completely different.

If the tortoise is free to roam amongst your flower beds be certain that your plants are protected. The way to do this is described in the next chapter. Not only may your plants and flowers be damaged but some of them may be harmful to the tortoise. Whilst on its travels your tortoise will no doubt consume quite large quantities of insects, snails, and worms; do not be alarmed by this habit as the roughage is essential to the animal's well-being. As mentioned earlier, tortoises are perpetual wanderers and for this reason they should be fed as early in the morning as possible. A hungry tortoise will travel quite some distance in order to find food, and this is usually how they get lost: if fed in the morning the tortoise will not have much inclination to travel and will merely fall asleep in some shady spot. It is fascinating to observe the tortoise's amazing sense of time, especially feeding time!

Most tortoises have different paths which they travel at the same time of day, day after day. If a number of tortoises are kept it will usually be found that they congregate at the feeding spot at the time they are due to be fed each day. This sense of timing is not restricted to the tortoise member of chelonia family, turtles are also known to do this and will swim excitedly back and forth in their tank when feeding time approaches. Food can be placed on the ground as long as it is free from dust and mud; vessels can be provided but it is usually difficult to find a suitable type from which the tortoise can easily feed. Being so clumsily built, the tortoise has to be stood over its food in order to reach it properly, with the result that a vessel or dish with a rim will usually be tipped up and a small tortoise may become trapped underneath. All animals need water in some form or another and this includes the tortoise. This is where a real difficulty arises with dishes: a suitable solution is to dig a hole in the ground and sink a shallow basin into it, but it must be one of the kind that will not rust. Tortoises are great lovers of bathing water and they will often sit in water for long periods soaking themselves. The sunken dish or basin should, therefore, be large enough to allow the tortoise to move about and climb in and out in complete safety. The level of the water will depend on the size of the tortoise using it. If the water is too deep the animal will drown, and if it is too shallow it will not be able to drink. A safe guide would be to ensure that the water level comes just below the edges of the plastron. Artificial bowls are best made from plastic as they are non-toxic and easily removed and cleaned out. If the tortoise-keeper likes to keep his garden looking smart and tidy then he can build his own pool from cement mortar. The ideal

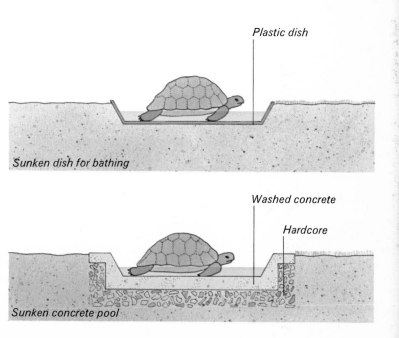

Plastic dish

Sunken dish for bathing

Washed concrete

Hardcore

Sunken concrete pool

size would be approximately 2 ft. in diameter and about 3 in. deep. When the cement is fully dry the pool should be filled with water and cleaned out before the tortoise is allowed to use it: cement contains certain alkalis which could be harmful to the skin and eyes of a tortoise. It is important to keep the drinking pool clean and never put food into it as the water will quickly stagnate and smell. If the simple rules of hygiene and common sense are followed, there should be no trouble in keeping the tortoise healthy and happy.

Housing

It is a fallacy to suggest, as many people do, that tortoises do not need any type of housing as they carry their own homes on their backs. In their natural habitat they will still seek shelter and warmth amongst the rocks and stones. Many thousands of pet tortoises are bought annually and when they arrive at their new home they are simply turned out into the garden to fend for themselves. Almost without exception they die, although some will live a little longer than others depending on the state of their health when first obtained from the wild. There is always a great cry of anguish when a dog, cat, or horse is treated cruelly by its owner. Very rarely is there the same reaction when it happens to the unfortunate tortoise. What can be more horrifying than being turned out into a garden with nowhere to shelter for the night? When the temperature drops to near freezing, as it does in many countries, the tortoise just freezes to death. Intentional cruelty is not the issue in these cases; it is just simple ignorance of the basic needs and necessities of the captive tortoise. Another equally cruel way of keeping the tortoise captive, practised far and wide, is to drill a hole in the carapace, near the tail, and thread string or twine through it in order to tie the animal to a stake driven into the ground. The shell is a living part of the tortoise itself and any unusual practices can only deform the animal and make it suffer.

To build a shelter to house a tortoise is both a simple and easy matter: any old wooden box can be used as long as three of the sides are solid and draught proof. The thickness of timber to be used can vary from $\frac{3}{8}$ in. to 1 in., but one must remember that the tortoise shelter has to last for quite some time and be able to withstand all types of weather.

The height inside the box will need to be about 3 in. higher than the tortoise shell, because if it is too low the tortoise may become jammed. Runners should be nailed along the bottom of the box in order to keep it off the ground; not only will this prevent the floor from becoming damp but it will also provide for a free flow of air to prevent the underside from becoming musty.

The whole interior can be painted with a lead-free paint, preferably emulsion, to brighten up the living quarter. The exterior should be painted with oil paint, preferably two coats, as this will help to protect the timber from the weather. When the paint is thoroughly dry the roof can be made waterproof; this can easily be done by obtaining a piece of roofing felt which must be at least

2 in. larger all the way round than the roof itself. When the felt is nailed into position it is a good idea to bend the edges downwards so that the rain will not run down the sides of the box and make it damp. The ideal solution here would be to purchase a suitably sized piece of corrugated perspex; this perspex could even replace the solid wooden roof, making viewing easy at all times. If this material proves too hard on the pocket then any piece of scrap metal can be used in its place, but it should be stressed that metal should not be used on its own: on a hot day it will turn the box into a furnace. Nail the metal to the existing wooden roof, making sure that any nails used in the construction are bent flat if they might cause injury to the tortoise. The front and doorway can be made next. To do this a space wider by half than the tortoise will need to be left at the front; both sides of the doorway can also be made from timber. For the sides, the coats of paint previously mentioned should be enough to protect them, but if further protection is required then they also can be covered with the same type of roofing felt as was used on the roof. The entrance must also be covered to prevent wind and driving rain from entering. This is best done by nailing a piece of material, which is both pliable and waterproof and will not rot, over the doorway, so it hangs down and completely covers the entrance. As the box or house is raised off the ground a way will have to be found to enable the tortoise to enter and leave it as it pleases. The most practical way to do this would be to make a wooden ramp for the tortoise to climb up. This ramp should have strips of wood nailed along it in a 'V' pattern, and there should be a gap of about $\frac{1}{2}$ in. at the base of the 'V' to enable soil and water to run away. The ramp should also be painted in the prescribed way for weather protection. The wooden house has the advantage that it is easily moved for cleaning purposes, and it is easy to maintain and keep in good order.

The next step is to find a suitable spot in which to site the tortoise house; it must be remembered that the box will only be used at night time when the temperature drops. It should not be placed where other household pets can upset it. As high a place as possible is beneficial because if placed in a hollow or depression the box may be in danger of becoming flooded during a rainstorm. It must also, of course, be easily accessible to the tortoise, whose home it is after all! There is no need to use any kind of bedding inside the tortoise house as the shell provides all the warmth the tortoise needs. The house is only to protect the animal from the elements.

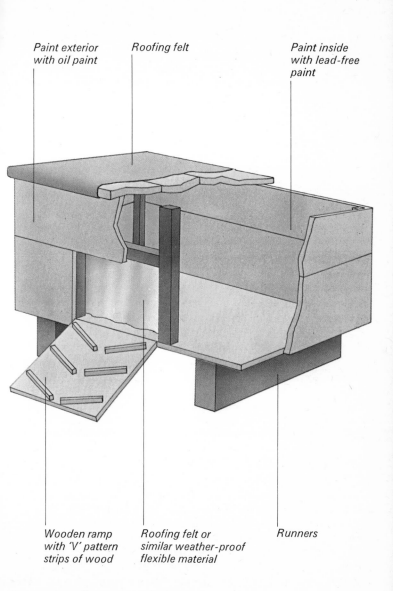

Paint exterior
with oil paint

Roofing felt

Paint inside
with lead-free
paint

Wooden ramp
with 'V' pattern
strips of wood

Roofing felt or
similar weather-proof
flexible material

Runners

An easy-to-make wooden tortoise-house

For the tortoise-keeper who prefers to make his tortoise-house a part of a well-kept garden there is the bunker type, which can either be concealed or made into a feature of the garden. The bunker structure is a permanent fixture and, therefore, requires much more care in its construction. The most convenient site for a house of this variety is in a bank of earth or a rockery. When the chosen site has been marked out the soil can be cut away and the base laid. To do this a layer of broken stones should be laid to a reasonable thickness and then cement poured over it and laid level with a straight piece of timber. The cement should contain small stone chippings or gravel as this will help to bind the cement together. Make sure the cement is not too thin or it may take too long to dry and be ruined by rain. Before the cement has had time to dry, a wooden box is placed in position on the wet concrete. The next step is to cover the walls of the box with a fairly stiff mixture of cement and gravel and, here again, if the mixture is too wet not only will it take a long time to dry but it will not stay in position and will simply slide down the walls. Whilst the walls are being plastered with cement the roof can also be treated in the same manner. A thickness of about 2 in. is advisable as this will not only take the weight of the earth that will be piled on it, but, to a certain extent, it will also protect the inside walls from dampness. As an additional protection from damp, the walls can be coated with a damp-proofing solution which can be bought from most paint stores and is usually specified for outside brick walls. When planning the site for the house it is absolutely essential that the entrance is at least 6 in. higher than the level of the lawn or path; if this is not done the inside of the house will be flooded when it rains. A ramp will now have to be made to enable the tortoise to enter and leave. This is best done by making a wooden frame or shutter and placing it in the position where the ramp is to be made. Simply fill in the frame with cement but instead of smoothing the surface, mark it with a pencil or stick in the 'V' formation, as described for the wooden ramp of the portable house. Once the cement is completely dry and quite hard the soil can be replaced. It is advisable to stamp the first few spadefuls to provide a firm surface. If the house has been set into a rockery, the stones can now be replaced and plants arranged to decorate the entrance.

The tortoise is by nature a great wanderer, so now our thoughts turn to protecting the plants and flower beds and filling any gaps in the garden fencing through which it might escape. Many tortoise-keepers think that a portable enclosure is the best way

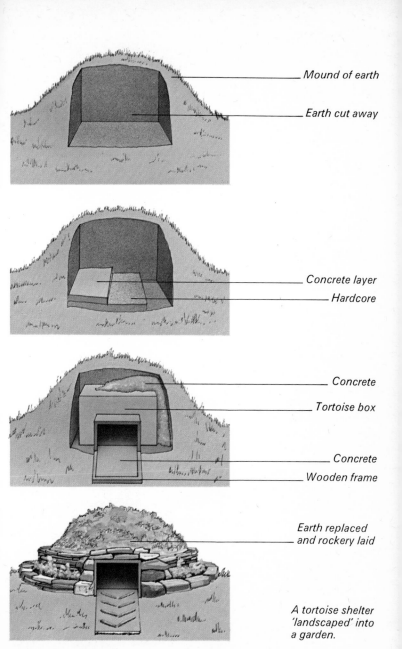

Mound of earth

Earth cut away

Concrete layer

Hardcore

Concrete

Tortoise box

Concrete

Wooden frame

Earth replaced
and rockery laid

*A tortoise shelter
'landscaped' into
a garden.*

25

of keeping the tortoise confined during the day. This idea is of course quite wrong as the tortoise needs plenty of freedom and minimal restrictions to keep him happy. The most effective way to protect flower beds is to build a small wire mesh fence around them, but if they are not erected in the right manner the fences will soon collapse with the weight of the tortoise in his untiring efforts to reach the plants on the other side. A trench will have to be dug at least 6 in. wide and 6 in. deep and then the fence posts should be driven into the ground at regular intervals along the full length of the intended fence. When the wire mesh is cut, allow at least 4 in. at the bottom and 2 in. at the top; this is to allow the wire to lie flat in the trench along the ground and also overhang at the top; if the tortoise cannot climb over the fence it will try to dig its way underneath it! The wire mesh is stretched across the fence posts and nailed into position, the trench is filled in, and the soil well trodden down. Having protected the garden and its contents we will now need to look at the existing fences and prevent any likely means of escape. By far the most effective method of fencing off any area is a brick wall. Those lucky enough to own a completely walled-in garden have no problem at all as usually the foundations are quite deep.

If a wire fence is already in use, the safest thing to do would be to take it down completely and erect a new one, which will have to be made in the same way as the one described for flower beds. The modern type of fence known as 'ranch style', and interwoven fencing present a different problem. Whilst they may be quite sound and strong they do not usually penetrate into the ground, and the tortoise will have no problems in quickly escaping. Here again the same type of wire guard as that used in the flower-bed fence can be employed, the only difference being that the edge of the wire can be nailed to the existing fence instead of using fence posts. It is a good idea to give the tortoise a patch of ground containing lettuce and other growing vegetables. Seeds can be sown at various stages of the year so that plants are always available.

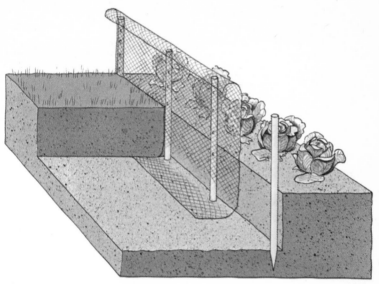

*A wire-mesh fence, constructed
and buried as shown, will provide
the necessary protection for your
plants from an exploring tortoise.*

General care

Most of the tortoises purchased as pets are usually bought for young children, and no real thought or consideration is given for the well-being of the animal. Before the tortoise is actually brought home, the basic housing requirements should be observed, as described in the previous chapter. It would be better not to purchase a tortoise at all if one is not prepared to give it a good home. Tortoises will live for a good number of years as long as they are looked after and kept healthy.

The tortoise is a reptile and therefore cannot regulate its body temperature in the same way as other living creatures. When tortoises are exported to another country they are subject to temperatures that are well below temperatures of their country of origin. Gradually they will acclimatize but this may take quite a few weeks. This problem does not arise in warmer countries of course, where there is generally a lower death rate in the pet tortoise.

If a diseased tortoise is included in an export consignment it will pass on the disease very quickly and so make the whole batch unhealthy. When actually buying a tortoise from a pet store there are one or two prime points to look for. The first is a pungent sour smell which will indicate a fungus growth or canker. The growth of this fungus usually affects the mouth and throat of the infected tortoise, with the result that the mouth cannot be clasped properly and the tortoise has difficulty in breathing. Unless the tortoise owner is prepared to give a lot of time to a sick animal, the diseased tortoise should be avoided. Running eyes are quite a common complaint and usually they are associated with a cold; with good management and proper feeding the cold will cure itself. Do not be hurried into a decision when selecting your pet; pick each one up and feel for the heavier specimens among the batch. The healthy tortoise should be quick moving and lively in its general appearance, it should have bright, clear eyes and a clean shell and limbs. The clean shell will indicate that the pet-store owner takes care of his stock and therefore one can usually assume that the tortoises he has for sale are in a healthy condition. The tortoise that is experiencing humans for the first time will of course be a little nervous and timid.

A tortoise that does not retract its head when handled is not necessarily tame, it is usually a sign of illness and this type should also be avoided. To test for good reflexes, pick up the tortoise; it should immediately retract its head and limbs. The hind legs

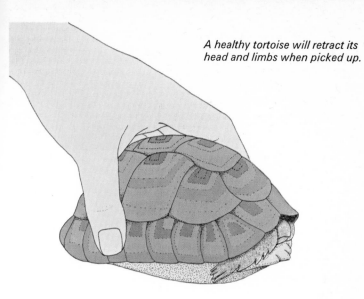

A healthy tortoise will retract its head and limbs when picked up.

may not retract but instead dangle freely; if this is so, touch the soles of the feet with a finger. The tortoise should push backwards and go into motions of walking. If the legs retract when pressure is applied this is yet another indication of ill health.

Whether a young tortoise is purchased in preference to an older one is entirely a matter of personal choice, but one must remember that young tortoises will need more looking after. Being less hardy, they are much more likely to be affected by colder climates and, if given the run of a garden, run the risk of becoming lost amongst the vegetation. The size of a tortoise does not indicate its age; older specimens usually have worn nails and the carapace is faded to some degree. Whenever possible a pair of tortoises should be obtained, as the company of another tortoise can cushion the feeling of strangeness after they are taken home. When children are allowed to handle tortoises, they should always be supervised by an adult. The tortoise is very strong for its size and can easily force itself free from the hand of a child. A tortoise will be lucky to survive a fall from a height: the carapace cannot stand a violent blow.

Hibernation

Hibernation is a very important part of the tortoise's life, and one that is little understood. During the summer months the tortoise is active and feeds readily, but as the winter draws near and the temperature starts to fall the tortoise slows down and its appetite diminishes. At this time good management is vital if the tortoise is to survive the winter. If the tortoise is left to wander in the garden it will eventually dig itself into the earth in a corner somewhere to hibernate until spring, but is unlikely to survive a hard frost.

It is a mistake to prevent an adult tortoise from hibernating as it will have eaten enough food during the summer to last it through the winter, and if it does not hibernate the tortoise will be overweight, and this could easily cause illness and even death. Instead the tortoise should be brought indoors to hibernate in a cool, dry place where there are no temperature fluctuations. The tortoise should be housed in a wooden or cardboard box filled with newspaper, straw, or any suitable litter; woodwool should not be used as this material has sharp edges which may cut the tortoise. Keep the box away from central-heating pipes or anything that may cause the temperature to rise. Garden sheds and garages make ideal hibernation quarters provided they are free from mice, rats, and any other vermin.

During hibernation the tortoise's respiration will slow down considerably and its breathing will become shallow. If the tortoise should wake up during the winter it should be fed for at least ten days and should not be returned to hibernation until the temperature has fallen. Sometimes a tortoise may end its hibernation a few months early. If this does happen it is best to keep the animal indoors until the outside temperature reaches a fairly constant level, and there is no danger of frost. The hibernation must never be forcibly ended by raising the temperature artificially as this sudden warmth may bring about undue dehydration which will be as fatal as the cold.

Great care must be taken with the tortoise when it does begin to awake. The eyes may become watery and sullen in appearance and they may prove difficult to open at first. A tepid solution of one part of boracic acid to five parts of water should be applied gently around the eyes to remove any pus. Food must of course be offered, but the tortoise may take from three to seven days to regain its appetite. Drinking water is essential to replace body moisture lost during hibernation.

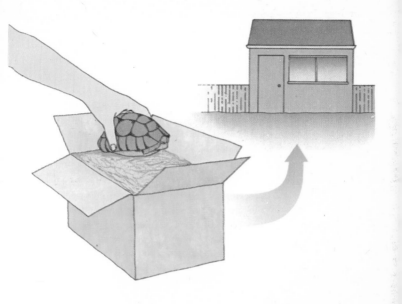

House a tortoise in a box with suitable bedding and keep in a shed for the hibernation period.

Illnesses

Soft shell

Soft shell is a marked softening of the bones and especially of the shell and is caused by a deficiency of calcium. The tortoise will refuse all food and will generally waste away. This illness affects young tortoises in particular, and lack of natural sunlight is one of the chief causes. If treatment is left too late a complete cure is almost impossible. The tortoise should be handled regularly as soft shell can usually be detected at the rear carapace (supracaudal) in the early stages.

The diet of a tortoise suffering from soft shell must be greatly enriched with vitamins C and D. This can best be done by offering the outer leaves of lettuce sprinkled with grated cuttlefish bone and, as soon as this is accepted, cod-liver oil and pure orange juice as well. Whenever the opportunity arises the sick animal should be placed in direct sunlight to help harden the shell by the intake of ultra-violet rays from the sun.

The cure is a slow one and if no progress is made after three to four weeks it would be advisable to have the tortoise destroyed. Calcium deficiency is the main cause of death in young pet turtles.

Colds

Newly imported tortoises are more susceptible to colds than are acclimatized specimens, although the cold will affect all kinds of captive chelonia. The indications of a developing cold are slight and not easily detected, but once the cold has taken hold the signs are unmistakable. The nose will discharge and the breathing become wheezy and laboured. This may be accompanied by running eyes and loss of appetite. The tortoise should be kept indoors at a temperature of 18°C–21°C. If breathing becomes very difficult a nasal ointment can be applied near the nostrils; only a small amount of ointment should be used: too much will cause discomfort.

The tortoise should be offered its favourite food and any delicacies that are usually offered only as a treat, and it must not be put outdoors until a complete cure is affected.

Worms

Worms affect almost all land-dwelling creatures but are not difficult to eradicate. Worms are in fact parasites and live in the bowel and intestine of their host; they are usually passed in the excreta and occasionally may be expelled from the mouth. There are two types of worm that affect tortoises: roundworm and ringworm. If a tortoise is seen to pass worms it should be isolated from its fellows and a proprietary worm expeller bought from a pet store. The instructions on the label should be followed until all signs of the parasites have vanished. Then and only then should the affected tortoise be allowed to mix with its fellows as worms are highly contagious. If a tortoise is found to have worms immediately prior to hibernation it should be treated in the prescribed manner until it is completely free of infection before it is allowed to hibernate.

Canker

Newly imported tortoises are again more susceptible to this disease. Canker is a very easily spread disease and should be treated with great respect. The symptoms are obvious and cannot be confused with anything else. The mouth and throat of the tortoise are affected by a strong-smelling growth, usually yellow in colour. If canker is detected during the early stages the cure is much easier and the disease less troublesome, but if the disease has taken a hold the growth will increase in size and in severe cases can choke its victim. Hence it is advisable to inspect the tortoise's mouth for canker at least once every month. Most pet stores sell a medicine that should be painted onto the growth. However, if the tortoise is in pain the kindest course is to have it destroyed.

Wounds

A reptiles skin, if damaged, is very slow to heal, and cuts therefore need careful treatment. Small cuts can be treated with a veterinary antiseptic ointment and covered with adhesive plaster. Larger wounds present a more difficult problem and, if care is not taken, can result in the loss of a limb. Continual bleeding is best stopped by constantly swabbing the wound with a piece of dry linen. A tourniquet should never be applied because there is a danger of causing permanent damage to vital cells and tissue. Once bleeding has stopped the wound should be bathed with a weak solution of antiseptic and water, and all traces of dirt removed. A dressing of clean linen is best as cotton wool tends to stick to the wound. It is impossible to prevent an active tortoise from moving, so the dressing will have to be secured with sticking plaster. As the dressing will soon become soiled it will have to be changed very regularly.

When the wound is completely dry and has started to heal, the dressing can be left off and ointment should be applied to the wound to protect it. The tortoise can then be allowed to wander indoors until the wound has healed completely. Terrapins and turtles must be kept out of water for a while after the application of ointment to allow it to take effect.

Parasites

Once again newly imported tortoises are most likely to be infected as the tortoise tick is usually present in quite large numbers in imported animals. The pet-store owner will usually try to make sure his tortoises are free of ticks but it would be very difficult to

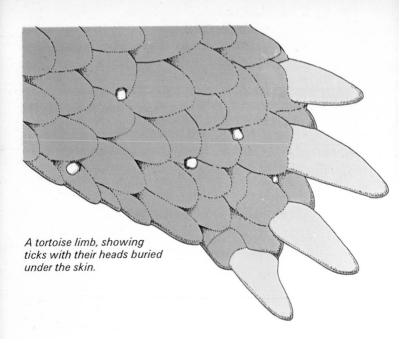

A tortoise limb, showing ticks with their heads buried under the skin.

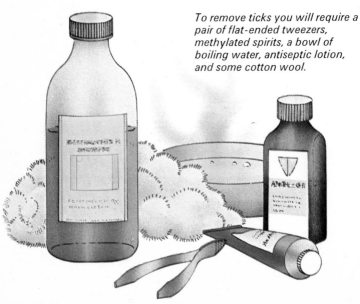

To remove ticks you will require a pair of flat-ended tweezers, methylated spirits, a bowl of boiling water, antiseptic lotion, and some cotton wool.

exterminate them completely.

When a tortoise is first brought home, inspect the shell thoroughly. Ticks can usually be detected between the skin and the shell, and will prove very difficult to remove unless the job is done correctly. The tick buries its head in the flesh of the tortoise leaving its body completely exposed. To be completely sure of extracting the whole of the parasite it should first be covered with a droplet of methylated spirits, then pulled out with a pair of flat-ended tweezers and dropped into a bowl of boiling water to which antiseptic has been added. The spots where the ticks were removed should be smeared with antiseptic lotion.

Breeding

The tortoise is one of the most difficult of all reptiles to breed in captivity. Even in these modern times little is really understood of the ways of their reproductive traits. Tortoises, like the majority of the reptile family, lay eggs, and these eggs differ slightly according to the particular species of tortoise. All tortoise eggs are white in colour although not all of them are hard-shelled; some of the tropical species lay eggs covered in a tough leathery skin. The various species also differ in the times of the mating season; the Mediterranean Spur Thighed Tortoise, for example, usually mates in the spring and summer, whilst the more tropical species, such as the Hercules Tortoise, mate in late autumn and winter.

The tortoise is usually thought of as a gentle and passive creature, but the male of the species can become quite aggressive towards his intended mate if she does not cooperate. A Common Greek Tortoise was once observed to perform a ritual dance when in pursuit of his intended mate but this single observation cannot be taken as characteristic of the species without further evidence. Once a male has singled out his intended mate from amongst the herd he will pursue her relentlessly. As the male nears the female he will butt her with his shell and try to bite her legs. A male Greek tortoise was observed to do this for over an hour, and during this time he did not once give up the chase. When the female finally submits she will remain still whilst the male climbs on her back and the sexual act is completed. During the act itself the male will utter a high-pitched scream.

The gestation period is quite long for so small an animal. No definite period has been recorded, but six months is not unusual and in the Giant Tortoise (*Testudo elephantopus*) periods of nine or ten months are common.

Pet tortoises that lay eggs in captivity are usually newly imported females which have mated before being captured. The female will show signs of becoming restless when she is due to lay her eggs. At first she may wander aimlessly and be unable to settle, then as the time approaches she will dig holes in the earth, one after the other, until finally she is satisfied that everything is in order, when she will dig the nest proper. The digging is done with the hind legs and during this process the female wets the inside of the hole with her own urine. This wetting of the earth serves two purposes: firstly, in the tortoises native land the earth is dry and the urine helps to bond the sides of the hole and prevent them from

A young tortoise breaks out of its shell.

falling in; secondly, a humid atmosphere is created as the sun warms the earth. When the nest is completed, the female backs over the entrance and proceeds to lay her eggs one at a time. The size of the clutch varies from species to species but there are usually between five and ten eggs. After laying her eggs the tortoise covers them with a thin layer of earth and urinates on them again, then covers the entrance completely to disguise the nest site. The tortoise has no maternal instinct and simply leaves the eggs to incubate. Again no definite period of incubation has been recorded.

As the tortoise embryo reaches full size within the egg it develops what is generally known as an egg tooth. This is not actually a tooth at all but an extension of the upper jaw similar to the beak of an eagle. When the young tortoise is ready to hatch it uses the egg tooth to break its way out of the shell, first piercing a hole in the shell and then gradually picking at the edges of the hole until it is large enough to crawl through. As the young tortoise grows the egg tooth will disappear and the scales of the limbs will start to form. The still soft shell of the young tortoise makes it very vulnerable to attack from predators and only the fittest will survive.

The hatching and rearing of captive tortoises is very difficult indeed, and anyone wishing to attempt it is advised to study the matter in some detail beforehand. Once the female has been seen to mate, a constant watch must be kept on her: if she lays her eggs unobserved it will be almost impossible to locate the nest. The female should not be disturbed in any way once the nest building has begun. When she has finally covered the nest, its position should be marked and it should be excavated as soon as possible, taking great care not to smash the eggs. When the eggs are removed they must be kept the same way up as they were in the nest, otherwise their chances of hatching will be seriously diminished. The top of each egg can be marked with a felt tip pen or similar marker, but not paint. An artificial incubator is required to accommodate the unearthed eggs. This must be made well in advance, for the eggs will perish if they are left for any length of time without sufficient heat and humidity. To make an incubator is a relatively simple matter, all one needs is a wooden box about 18 in. square, which can be made from scrap timber, or even a cut-down tea chest. Fine sand is then laid in the bottom to a depth of 6 in.; ordinary earth is too thick in texture for this purpose.

If the eggs are to stand any chance of hatching they will have to be kept at a fairly constant temperature. It would be of no use placing the box in an airing cupboard because the temperature fluctuations would be too great. The best method is to provide artificial heat, and this is easy to install. A wooden lid should be made to fit over the top of the incubator, but it must not be too tight otherwise the flow of air will be restricted. A hole is drilled through the lid and through this is passed an electric lead. A lampholder is fixed to the end inside the box and to a suitable plug the other end.

The best type of lamp to use is a 40 watt to 60 watt filament lamp; fluorescent tubes do not give off the required amount of heat, with the exception of the 'Growlux' type used to rear tropical plants, which is obtainable in some tropical-fish shops. It has been suggested that the eggs of certain species of tortoise are sensitive to light and as a precaution a red- or orange-coloured lamp should be used. If a coloured lamp cannot be obtained, an ordinary lamp can be painted with emulsion paint without affecting the heat given off. A thermometer should be placed inside the incubator so that the temperature can be checked. The eggs are best kept at a temperature of about 26°C. and the lamp will have to be raised or

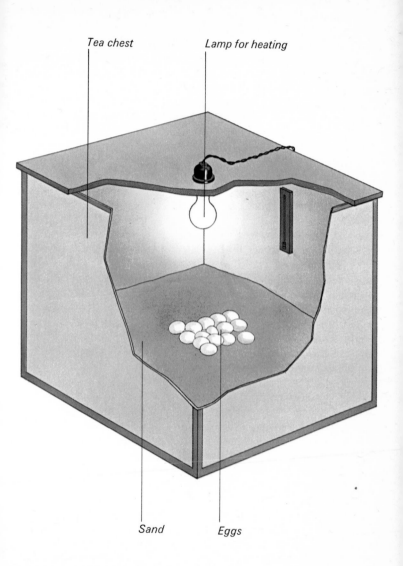

Tea chest

Lamp for heating

Sand

Eggs

An incubator

lowered until this level is reached. The wire can then be held in place with a clip on the lid. The eggs should be placed on the sand in the incubator the same way up as they were found in the nest, then covered with more sand until they are about ½ in. below the surface. The sand should be lightly sprayed with tepid water to create a small amount of humidity. The eggs must not now be disturbed under any circumstances. All that needs to be done is to ensure that the lamp stays lit, and perhaps lightly spray the sand with water about once every fourteen days; do not soak the sand as this would cause too much humidity and the eggs might rot. Tortoise eggs have been hatched without any additional spraying so this is a matter of personal choice.

When the tortoise eggs are due to hatch they will slowly work their way up to the surface of the sand until they are in full view. Hatching is a strenuous process for the baby tortoise, and may take from two to twenty-four hours. If a baby tortoise is well nourished and strong it may hatch without any particular effort. If one seems to be in difficulty, tweezers can be used to remove pieces of the shell until the animal can escape, but great care must be taken. The newly hatched tortoise will still be attached to the albumen of the egg. Do not attempt to touch this in any way but leave it to dry off naturally; this may take a few days. When hatched and dry, the baby tortoise will be fully developed, although the shell and limbs may be rubbery in appearance and without the scale of the mature adult.

The baby tortoises must be kept warm in order to stimulate feeding and growth, and this raises the question of housing the babies. A special type of cage for reptiles, called a vivarium, can be bought from a pet store. These are usually made of metal, but there is no reason why one should not be made out of wood. Fish tanks, because they do not allow an adequate flow of air, are not recommended. The bigger the vivarium the better, but an ideal floor size is about 12 in. by 18 in. Most vivariums have a light fitting included, but in any case one can easily be installed. The front has an upper removable glass panel. The lower part of the front is also removable to provide access for cleaning. One side of the vivarium has a gauze-covered window to provide a flow of air. The temperature inside the vivarium should be between 21°C and 26°C, certainly not lower than this, and must be kept constant. Fine sand can be used as a floor dressing and this must be changed regularly. During the night the babies will need some shelter from the glare of the light; a small upturned cardboard box

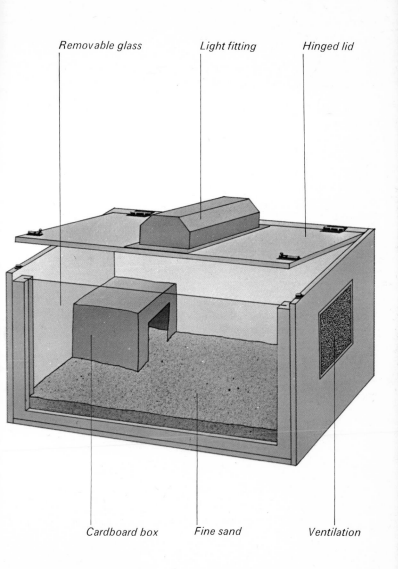

Removable glass   Light fitting   Hinged lid

Cardboard box   Fine sand   Ventilation

A vivarium for baby tortoises

will provide this. Water must be provided at all times, and must be changed regularly.

A newly hatched tortoise will usually show no interest in food, and may refuse to eat for up to a week. The diet should consist of soft food for at least the first twelve months of life. Crushed grapes, tomato, apple, orange, banana can be offered, and lettuce should be provided to give roughage. Food should not be left in the vivarium long enough for it to wilt and go sour.

The vivarium must be placed in a draught-proof place that receives a good deal of sunlight from a window. Ivor Noel-Hume in his book *Tortoises* describes an experiment in which two baby tortoises from a brood of five were kept away from sunlight and given only artificial light. Their shells became soft, due no doubt to the lack of ultra-violet rays from the sun, and they died within six months. Glass has the tendency to filter out ultra-violet rays, but some get through and are enormously beneficial to the well-being of a young tortoise. Whenever possible the young tortoises should be given the opportunity to bathe in direct sunlight, but the temperature inside the vivarium must not be allowed to drop below 21 °C.

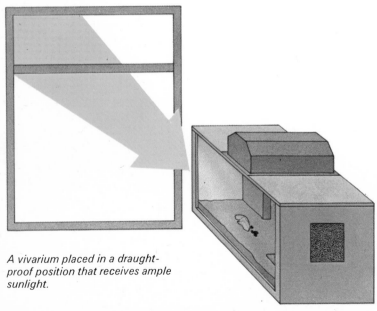

A vivarium placed in a draught-proof position that receives ample sunlight.

The growth of the young tortoise is very slow indeed, and not at all uniform. Some may put on weight very quickly whilst their brothers and sisters stay the same weight and size for a long time. Some may reach a length of 6 in. at four years of age, others only 4 in. The carapace is measured to determine the length of the tortoise, the plastron usually being slightly shorter. Young tortoises should never be left at night in the garden until they measure 4 in.–6 in. and even then they should not be allowed to experience temperatures lower than 10°C. During the summer, tortoises of this size can be placed in a home-made run in the garden, in a spot where the sun shines for most of the day. Winter time must of course be spent indoors. Young tortoises under 4 in. in length should not be allowed to hibernate as this can be very detrimental to their health.

Species

There are approximately 250 known species of tortoise, and they are to be found in all parts of the world, except those with colder climates. Most of the Chelonia family are found in tropical areas, which provide plenty of cover in which to hide. Though the tortoise is one of the oldest species of animal, very little is understood of its ways and breeding habits. It is secretive by nature and can only be observed in the wild state with great patience,

Most species were discovered many years ago but not until 1953 was the Short-Necked Tortoise of Australia discovered, and then quite by accident. A tortoise in a pet show at a fair was found to have a much shorter neck than its fellow exhibits. The boy who owned the tortoise explained that it was found in a local swamp, but it was taken to be an escaped imported tortoise. It was not until the curator of a local museum became interested that another specimen was found and the species identified.

The Giant Galapagos Tortoise, on the other hand, has been known for many hundreds of years and thanks to man's selfish ways nearly became extinct. As this species is unique, it will be dealt with in the following chapter. It would be an impossible task to describe all the known species of tortoise and so only the most well known will be mentioned.

Greek Tortoise *(Testudo gracea; Testudo herrmani)*

The term Greek Tortoise is applied to a variety of tortoise that is found around the shores of the Mediterranean. The two main species are the Spur Thighed Tortoise and the Herrmans Tortoise. The only difference between the two species is that the aptly named Spur Thighed Tortoise has a horny projection on each hind leg, while the Herrmans Tortoise has a hooked claw on the tail. The Spur Thighed variety live chiefly in Tunisia and Morocco, but can also be found as far away as Spain, Greece, Israel, and Turkey. The colour of the carapace varies from region to region but usually has a yellowish-brown ground colour with black markings on each carapace plate. The two species are amongst the easiest of the Chelonia family to look after. The male tortoise usually has a slightly longer tail than the female and the plastron is slightly concave. Both species grow to about 1 ft. long and have similar breeding habits. Mating occurs in the early spring and the eggs are laid in June, an average clutch consisting of about ten eggs. The eggs are white and hard-shelled and in their natural habitat they are incubated by the warmth of the sun.

Greek Tortoise   *Testudo gracea; Testudo herrmani*

Carolina Box Tortoise *(Terrapene carolina carolina)*
This is the common tortoise of the United States, and is found in nearly all the warmer states. There are several subspecies and these can only be distinguished by close inspection. The two other main species are the Three Toed Box Tortoise and the Ornate Box Tortoise.

The Carolina Box Tortoise has a highly domed carapace for such a small animal. The ground colour is usually dark brown and sometimes may appear black, with yellow spots or marks. The yellow-ochre plastron has a unique hinged forepart which, when fully retracted, completely hides the head of the tortoise. The average size of the Carolina Box Tortoise is usually 6 in.–8 in., although it has been known to grow much larger in Florida. The sexes are easily distinguishable by the fact that the adult male has red eyes whereas the female's eyes are a greyish-blue.

The Three-Toed Box Tortoise, which inhabits the states just north of Mexico, is much smaller than its Carolina cousin but is coloured in much the same way. As its name suggests it has only

Carolina Box Tortoise   *Terrapene carolina carolina*

Three-toed Box Tortoise   *Terrapene carolina triunguis*

three toes instead of the customary four. The 4 in.–5 in. long plastron has the unique hinge of the Carolina species. Both these species mate around April to May and the very thin, hard-shelled white eggs are laid in July.

The Ornate Box Tortoise is found further south than the other species of box tortoise, in the states of Dakota, Texas, Wyoming, Iowa, and as far south as the Mexican border. It prefers dry, shady regions and can go without water for some considerable time. The carapace is very similar to that of Carolina species but has a reddish-brown ground colour with the same yellow spots and markings; these also cover the limbs. The shell is not quite as high and the eye colour is not the same as in the Carolina species.

Box Tortoises are easy to keep as pets, but in colder climates they should be kept indoors during cold weather. All three species are omnivorous, that is they eat both meat and vegetable matter, and a diet of meat scraps and fruit and vegetables should be offered. Meal-worms can be given occasionally as they have a high protein content. The hibernation period is from October to May.

Gopher Tortoise *(Gopherus polyphemus)*
This is another North American species of tortoise and is found in the states of Louisiana, Alabama, Florida, and Georgia. It is one of the largest of the American tortoises and can reach a length of 1 ft. when fully adult. The plastron is a dull, dark brown all over with no identification marks, but has the unusual feature of an extension just under the neck, which is sometimes used as a levering device to topple an opposing male during a fight.

The Gopher Tortoise prefers pine woods and sandy hills in which to make its home. Secretive by nature, it lives in burrows by day and emerges at nightfall to feed. In captivity the tortoise should be fed on a varied diet of fruit and greenfood and should be provided with sandy soil in which to dig and hide, fine sand should not be used as this may collapse and suffocate the animal.

Desert Tortoise *(Gopherus agassizi)*
The Desert Tortoise is a close relative of the Gopher Tortoise, but lacks the plastron spur of the latter. It is found in hot desert areas, and is especially abundant in the Majave desert, California. It is similar in size and shape to the Gopher Tortoise. However, it does not dig burrows but shelters from the heat of the day by lying in the shade of a rock or boulder. It feeds on vegetation during the spring and the rainy season, and lies torpid during the hot summer ; this is an exact reversal of the hibernation of other species. Desert tortoises are very difficult to keep in captivity as humid conditions seem to upset them, and they may die after only a short time.

Berlandiers Tortoise *(Gopherus berlandieri)* Texas Tortoise (U.S.A.)
Yet another of the genus of Gopher Tortoise, this species is closely related to the Desert Tortoise but has a slightly domed carapace, instead of the low flat shell of the other species. Berlandiers Tortoise is limited to central Texas and northern Mexico. Its overall colour is slightly lighter than that of the Desert Tortoise but it is about the same length (1 ft.).

Brazilian Giant Tortoise *(Testudo denticulata)*
Although not a true Giant Tortoise in the true sense of the word, the Brazilian Tortoise is certainly one of the largest of the Chelonia race ; and can reach a length of 2 ft. when fully adult.

The carapace is very narrow compared with its length and is very low-slung. The true carapace colour is actually yellow but

48

Gopher Tortoise   *Gopherus polyphemus*

most specimens have brown pigmentation which makes the carapace very dark. It has a number of other names, the most common being Red-legged Tortoise, Red-headed Tortoise, and Hercules Tortoise. Individuals vary considerably in their markings; some have orange heads whilst others may have red. On the legs the prominent scales are usually orange and black though they may sometimes appear red.

In its wild state the Brazilian Tortoise inhabits thick jungle areas. It feeds on a wide variety of soft fruits and vegetation and is therefore easy to feed in captivity. It is not a great lover of the sun, but in captivity it must be encouraged to take some fresh air if it is to remain healthy. This tortoise has never been known to breed in captivity, although several attempts have been made.

The Leopard Tortoise *(Testudo pardalis)*
This is perhaps the best known of all the African species, and one of the largest. It is a native of South Africa and Abyssinia. The species is aptly named, for the carapace has a ground colour of yellow which is mottled with black. The very high dome of the carapace has large plates, which afford the animal very good protection. The usual length is 7 in. but specimens have been known to grow to 18 in.

The Leopard Tortoise is a great sun lover and can withstand very high temperatures. In captivity the temperature must never be allowed to drop below 15°C. or the animal will cease to feed and great difficulty may be encountered in coaxing it to start again. The diet is very extensive and although some specimens may prefer vegetables to fruit and vice versa, almost all the foods already mentioned will be readily taken. The only drawback with keeping the Leopard Tortoise as a pet is its great appetite, which can make it expensive to feed. Breeding in captivity is relatively easy provided climatic and environmental conditions are favourable.

South African Starred Tortoise *(Testudo tentoria)*
This species is found in all parts of South Africa and has many closely linked species and subspecies. The highly domed carapace can reach a length of 8 in. and is very decorative in its markings. The ground colour varies from a very light yellow to ochre and is sharply contrasted by blotches of dark brown and black which leave only fine radiating lines of the yellow ground colour visible — hence the name 'starred'. The plastron is also yellow with a dark-

Leopard Tortoise   *Testudo pardalis*

brown line running the full length of the body. Like the Leopard Tortoise, the Starred Tortoise requires constant high temperatures if it is to thrive in captivity. Food is again an easy matter as it will eat almost anything and will readily accept mealworms as a tit-bit.

Geometric Tortoise *(Testudo geometrica)*
This species is closely related to the Starred Tortoise, the main difference being the colour of the carapace, which has an identical starred pattern. This pattern extends onto the plastron. The diet is the same as for the Starred Tortoise, and the same climatic conditions are required in captivity.

Kuhl's Tortoise *(Testudo oculifera)*
This is yet another subspecies of *Testudo tentoria*, with the difference that the carapace has a serrated edge that gives the effect of a frill. The carapace is also not as highly domed as in its cousins and the markings are very much paler in colour. Kuhl's Tortoise comes from the drier, sandy areas of South Africa and is much sought after for its shell; these are sold as cigarette boxes in souvenir shops, a trade which must be halted if the species is not to become extinct.

Angulated Tortoise *(Testudo angulata)*
Although not related to the starred varieties of African tortoise, the Angulated Tortoise has the same carapace pattern, but this is much less marked and in some specimens is nearly invisible. The yellow plastron has a blunt projection just underneath the neck. The carapace is low and about 6 in. long. One unusual feature of this species is its very long neck which can reach a distance of 4 in. The Angulated Tortoise has very rarely been kept in captivity, and its diet and climatic likes and dislikes have not yet been established.

Eroded Cinixys Tortoise *(Cinixys erosa)*
This species lives in the jungle areas of Africa and is perhaps the most unusual of all the African tortoises. The yellow carapace is marked with brown and in some specimens will appear entirely brown with no ground colour showing at all. The near marginals have serrated edges. The familiar hinge of the Cinixys species is located towards the hind limbs and tail, but is rarely used. The plastron has a forked projection on which the animal rests its head when sleeping. The head is bright yellow and very pointed.

Eroded Cinixys Tortoise   *Cinixys erosa*

When angered or excited the tortoise walks with a high stepping motion on its long, thin legs, raising itself some distance from the ground. In captivity it prefers a diet of soft fruit and vegetables and dislikes strong sunlight. It should be kept away from other species as it is aggressive by nature and will attack with the slightest provocation.

Bells Cinixys Tortoise *(Cinixys belliana)*

This species sometimes displays the starred effect of *Testudo geometrica* but its more usual appearance is similar to that of *Cinixys erosa.* It is, however, easily distinguishable from *Cinixys erosa* by its long narrow carapace and its much smaller size of 5 in. Bells Cinixys also lacks the serrated edges of the near marginals seen in *Cinixys erosa.* Bells Cinixys comes from the more northerly areas of Africa and requires higher temperatures if kept in captivity.

Radiated Tortoise *(Testudo radiata)*

This highly decorative species is a native of the island of Madagascar. Once again the starred pattern is present in the carapace markings and is very highly contrasted by a yellow-orange ground colour. Unlike the South African Starred Tortoise, the Radiated species has a low smooth carapace and is much longer (about 18 in.). Fruit makes up the main part of this tortoise's diet although it will also eat vegetables and small pieces of meat.

Indian Starred Tortoise *(Testudo elegans)*

This species of Starred Tortoise is the most common of the imported tropical varieties. It is widespread over India and Ceylon, and inhabits regions varying from jungle to dry sandy terrain. The delicate starred pattern is achieved in the same way as the African species with a vivid-yellow ground broken by dark-brown, almost black triangular markings. The pattern also extends onto the plastron as in *Testudo geometrica.* The main difference between the African and Indian species is that the Indian species has conically shaped vertebrals, which give it an even more decorative appearance. Fully mature specimens may reach a length of 8 in. The Indian Starred Tortoise is easy to keep in captivity and is an ideal family pet. It can be fed on almost all the previously mentioned foods.

Bells Cinixys Tortoise   *Cinixys belliana*

Indian Starred Tortoise   *Testudo elegans*

Burmese Tortoise *(Testudo platynata)*

The Burmese Tortoise is not related to the Indian Tortoise, and is much smaller, rarely exceeding 6 in. The main difference in the two species lies in the smaller triangular markings on the carapace of the Burmese species, which give thicker radiating lines. The flat vertebral plates of the Burmese Starred Tortoise are another distinguishing feature. Captive conditions are the same as for the Indian Starred Tortoise.

The Giant Tortoise

Whenever one visits a zoo one of the main attractions is often the Giant Tortoise, a relic of a bygone age. There are two species of Giant Tortoise, the Galapagos Tortoise, U.S.A.: Elephant Tortoise, *(Testudo elephantopus)* and the Seychelle Tortoise *(Testudo gigantica)*, sometimes referred to as the Indian Ocean Giant Tortoise. The prehistoric tortoise of the Asian continents, *Colosochelys atlas*, was the first of the Giant species and today's Giant Tortoises have changed very little from their primitive ancestors. It is remarkable that both species inhabit remote islands and it is not certain how they managed to get there in the first place. One feasible explanation is that they were carried from the mainland clinging to pieces of driftwood as it has been proved that tortoises can float and survive in water for long periods.

As mentioned in Chapter I, the sailors of the eighteenth century who had to rely on salted meat and water for the main part of their

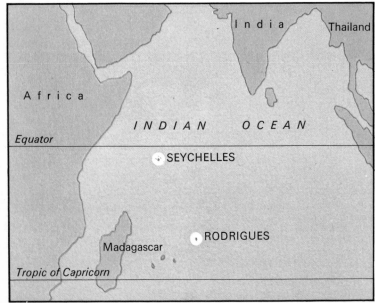

Wholesale slaughter of the Giant Tortoise by eighteenth-century sailors led to this creature's virtual extinction in certain parts of the world. The Island of Rodriguez was among the first places to suffer. Farms, such as those in the Seychelles, were set up to conserve the Giant Tortoise.

diet, found in the Giant Tortoise a welcome supply of fresh meat. The creatures were driven in their hundreds aboard ships and killed and eaten when they were needed. This wholesale slaughter very soon diminished their numbers with the result that many previously populated areas became devoid of tortoise life. The Island of Rodriguez was perhaps the first to suffer in this way. In eighteen months the whole population of tortoises was completely wiped out, due mainly to the fact that a penal colony was established there by the French, and what remained of the tortoises was finished off completely to provide meat for the prisoners.

Many scientists and naturalists have studied the Giant Tortoises, notably Charles Darwin who was fascinated by them and their habits. By the end of the nineteenth century the Galapagos Tortoise was in danger of complete extinction, and it is due to the efforts of zoologists that we can still see them today. In the Seychelles, farms were set up to promote and conserve the Giant Tortoise and as many adults as possible were collected.

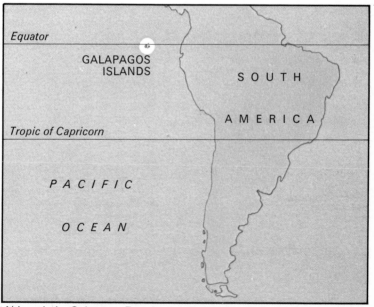

Although the Galapagos Tortoise, studied by Darwin in the mid nineteenth century, was threatened with extinction by the end of that century, the efforts of zoologists averted disaster.

Breeding the Giant Tortoise has always been difficult but steps are being made in the right direction, as the following article, from the *International Zoo Yearbook,* number 9, shows. Written by Jack Throp it relates the great care and attention these animals receive at the zoo where Mr. Throp is director.

In 1965 a project was begun to search out the hidden factors in establishing a consistent reproduction programme with the Honolulu Zoo's herd of Galapagos Tortoise, consisting of seven adult males and five adult females. In the early days of their captivity we had some trouble with their digestion and their faeces were watery and smelly; not like the compact stool as described for the animals in the wild. The diet was improved by adding course roughage to the fare of lettuce, cabbage and fruit. Pineapple tops were tried but they fermented rapidly and no practical method of storage could be devised. However, large pellets are made locally from them as a roughage supplement for dairy cattle and these were added to the diet. Banana stalks and palm leaves were also given.

The original enclosure was 69 ft. by 174 ft. of flat denuded hard-packed soil. A further area, which is about twice as large and grass covered, has now been added. This allows the tortoises to obtain extra roughage and, of course, gives better opportunities for exercise. In this enclosure a mud hole has been made for the males. This is about 2 ft. deep and 3 ft. across and is kept filled with water. For several months all the males and several of the females slept in it. It was felt that the water and soft bottom would make it easier for the animals to breathe and possibly improve the fertility of the males. Attempts at mating were carried on throughout the year and it was thought that this might be too much of a good thing. It was apparent that though the males persisted, the females were not receptive and just clamped their bodies to the ground. No successful mating was seen in more than one year of observation. For this reason the sexes were separated in October 1966 and reunited six months later. The females were then seen to rear up on their hind legs and successful mating was possible. In 1967 two clutches of eggs were recovered. A third clutch of at least nine eggs were destroyed by a female as she covered the nest.

The tortoise nest is dug by the use of alternate hind legs and is somewhat bell shaped, larger at the bottom than at the throat of the hole. They apparently prefer clay or compact soil in which to make their nests, and in the enclosure used an area where the soil and volcanic ash have combined to make an adhesive but pliable soil when wet. Furthermore the hole is wetted by the female releasing urine from the bladder as she digs. When the hole is about 8 in.–10 in. deep she backs over it and drops the eggs singly in batches with a short pause between each batch. Each egg is nearly spherical in shape, hard shelled and a little over 2 in. in diameter. After laying, the female pushes some of the soil in on top of the eggs and compresses it with somewhat rotary motions of her body. The finished result is a well-disguised nest site.

The first clutch recovered consisted of 16 eggs, the second 11 eggs. In removing the eggs it was found that the nest was hollow and contained an air pocket which retains most of the moisture deposited by the female. Hendrickson (1959) believes that the Galapagos tortoise eggs can be moved safely only up to 3 days after laying, after that time the viable eggs would be

Galapagos Tortoise, U.S. : Elephant Tortoise   *Testudo elephantopus*

destroyed by disturbance. An artificial incubator chamber was created using a large cement pot. Four inches of soil from the nest was placed in the bottom, after the container itself was saturated with water. The eggs were placed carefully one upon the other in the same manner as they were deposited by the female. The opening was then sealed with glass and black tar paper.

It was felt that the embryos might be light sensitive though this was only an assumption. The incubating temperature was kept at a fairly constant 28°C–25°C. Some three and a half months after the setting of the first clutch of 16 eggs it was discovered that 13 had hatched, but probably due to the activity of the new born, one of the infertile eggs had exploded, flies had been attracted through an imperfect seal on the glass top and their larvae had destroyed the entire clutch. The incubation period had been approximately 106 days. The second clutch of 11 eggs had fared better and nine hatched on the 96th day of incubation. It is interesting that the incubation periods at San Diego Zoo had varied markedly from 161 to 246 days. From an attempted incubation 258 eggs, San Diego Zoo has hatched 17 young tortoises, with ten dead embryos. The fertility percentage was thus 10.24 per cent with 6.97 per cent of eggs actually hatching. In 1967 we incubated 27 eggs and hatched 22 showing 81.48 per cent fertility and 100 per cent viable egg hatch.

We created a protected environment for the young. This was a large indoor planter box that had been tufted with a dense growth of Bermuda Grass. One corner of the 9 in. × 9 in. box was kept clear and the food was placed there. Artificial light was used as a source of heat. The box provided ample hiding areas and retreats for the nervous young and 24-hour warmth and light. A finely grained lettuce, locally called Monoa lettuce, was fed, as well as Papaya and apple. A vitamin mineral compound and scraped cuttlefish bone was sprinkled on the food. The second week mealworms were tried and the young actually sought them out from amongst the vegetables. From this it was obvious that they needed more protein than we thought. Ground horsemeat was added to the diet and later canned dog meat. All were readily accepted and were eaten before the vegetables. An outdoor box was made for the young tortoises to bask in the sun.

From this experience it is thought possible for the tortoise to be capable of reproduction in large numbers if proper care is given.

Just as in fishing stories, there have been many exaggerated tales of the size of Giant Tortoises. When the sailors of the eighteenth century returned home they told tales of seeing tortoises that were 10 ft. or more in length. The more usual size of the Giant Tortoise is about 4 ft. long and 2 ft.–3 ft. wide. When walking the animal lifts itself clear of the ground and reaches a height of 3 ft. from the ground to the top of its shell. The carapace is very smooth and a uniform brown all over. The most striking difference between the Galapagos species and the Indian Ocean Giant Tortoise is the make-up of the carapace. Both are of the same brown colour but in the Galapagos Tortoise the carapace has a much more spherical shape, while the carapace of the Indian Ocean Tortoise is indented

Seychelle Tortoise   *Testudo gigantica*

in places, giving it a bumpy appearance. The margin between the carapace plates is much finer in the Indian species and the shell itself is much smoother and more finely grained. The Galapagos Giant Tortoise, on the other hand, has wide channels between each carapace plate and the texture of the shell is not unlike that of the hide of a rhinocerus.

When fully distended the necks of both species can reach a length of 2 ft. This is very useful to the animal in its native surroundings as it feeds on a wide variety of plants, fruits, and other types of vegetation, including cactus, which it consumes without ever seriously harming its face. Soon after the rainy season the Galapagos Tortoise descends from its native hills to feed on the lush green plains, and when the long, hot summer begins to dry up the lower vegetation, it returns to feed once again on the mountain pastures.

One of the most remarkable aspects of the Giant Tortoise is its enormous longevity. It is very difficult to establish the exact age of a specimen in the wild state, and even in captivity no definite proof has ever been available to substantiate the age of a particular long-lived specimen. The oldest tortoise to be regularly observed is Samir of Cairo Zoo, Egypt, who is reputedly 273 years old.

Turtles and terrapins

This book would seem incomplete without some mention of the sea-going turtle and its close relative, the fresh-water terrapin. The word terrapin is derived from a North American Indian word *terrapene,* and the terms turtle and terrapin are frequently synonymous. Turtles are zoologically classed in the same order, Chelonia, as tortoises, but whereas the tortoise in the process of evolution became a land-dweller, the turtle remained an aquatic creature, though some species of turtles are as much at home on land as they. are in the water. In its adaptation to the sea the turtle has developed flippers instead of claws although the nails are still present. In South Africa fossils were found of a prehistoric turtle named Eunotosaurus, which is the forebearer of the species found today. There are approximately fifty species of turtle, found in nearly every part of the world. They range in size from the large sea-going Heatherback and Green Turtles to the tiny Mud and Red Eared Terrapins.

Unfortunately when one mentions the word turtle the culinary dish of turtle soup instantly springs to mind; turtles are all too often referred to as the 'gourmets' delight'. The substance sold commercially as 'tortoiseshell' is in fact the shell of the unfortunate turtle, whose body is used to make the soup. Turtle eggs, too, are regarded as a delicacy in many parts of the world. At one time these eggs were taken in such large numbers that a sharp decrease in the world's turtle population resulted. Although the eggs are still collected they are done so under license with strict control.

Unlike the tortoise, in which the shape of the carapace differs from species to species, all species of turtle possess a flat smooth shell and streamlined body contours, which are well suited to an aquatic life. The carapace of a turtle is usually soft and pliable, which reduces the dead weight of the animal and makes it buoyant in the water, and the limbs of the turtle have been adapted to form flippers. The front flippers have an action reminiscent of a bird's wings in flight, with upward and backward and downward and forward movements. The hind flippers are used as rudders to guide the body in the right direction.

It is interesting to note that fresh-water terrapins do not swim in the same way as the sea-going species of turtle. The terrapin's movements are more of a paddling action, much less graceful but just as effective. The turtle's front flippers can be likened to the wings of an aeroplane with a thick leading edge and fine trailing

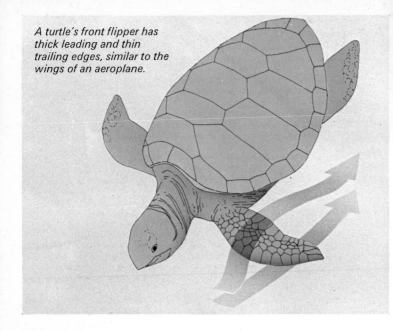

A turtle's front flipper has thick leading and thin trailing edges, similar to the wings of an aeroplane.

edge. On shore the turtle has a slow-moving and awkward gait. The Green Turtle pushes and pulls itself along with the rear and fore limbs in unison, while the Loggerhead and Hawksbill species use more orthodox crawling movements.

Female turtles have been said to cry when they come ashore to lay their eggs. This effect is due to excess salt being repulsed from the body. Sea-going turtles take in much more salt than their bodies actually need, and the excess is dispelled from ducts next to the turtles' eyes.

Turtles breathe air in the same way as tortoises, and when submerged they need to hold their breath for quite some time. To do this the turtle has developed a unique way of supplying only the most important tissues and organs with oxygen when submerged, thus making one breath of air last much longer. Like tortoises, turtles all need to bask in the sun in order to absorb the ultra-violet rays containing vitamin D, which is so vital to strong and healthy bones. Heat is also vital to these cold-blooded creatures; without it they would be unable to digest their food and would not grow at the normal rate.

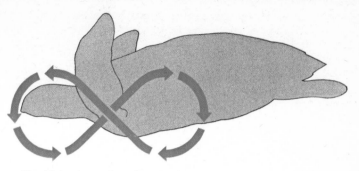

The bird-wing action of sea turtles.

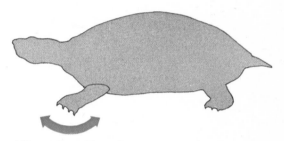

The paddling action of terrapins.

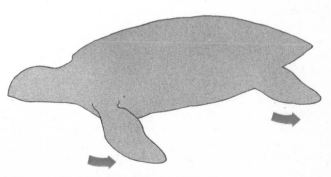

The unorthodox push-pull action of the Green turtle.

After digging a hole, the turtle lays a clutch of 140 eggs.

Every species of terrapin, turtle, and tortoise lay eggs. In order to maintain a steady number of mature adults turtles lay large numbers of eggs, for young turtles have many enemies and only a very small percentage ever reach maturity. The female turtle comes ashore at night to deposit her eggs in the sand out of reach of the tide. It may take an hour for her to drag herself slowly and laboriously up the beach to the dry sand. Digging a hole in the sand is also a slow and painstaking process. The flippers act as scoops and each hind flipper scoops out sand in the same way as a human hand. When satisfied with the hole, the female turtle will commence to lay her eggs. The eggs are deposited two, three, and sometimes four at a time. Green Turtles lay an average of 140 eggs in each clutch, and this process may take up to two hours. The sand that was dug out is then carefully replaced and the nest is concealed by dragging the hind flippers over the surface of the nest in a side-to-side movement. Turtle eggs take about six weeks to hatch. As they become ready for hatching they are propelled upwards through the sand until they are just below the surface, when hatching commences.

The nesting and egg-laying process is the same in terrapins as it is in turtles except that the terrapin, being a freshwater species, lays its eggs in mud and soft earth. The young of both species face the same hazards when they emerge from the nest. As soon as they hatch, the young run for the comparative safety of the water, but many never reach it because of marauding birds and animals. Once in the water they are the prey of carnivorous fish and, in the case of the sea turtle, the shark.

Young turtles require an enormous amount of food in order to maintain a steady growth rate: from hatching to maturity the turtles have to increase their body size some 2,000 times.

Turtle species

Green Turtle *(Chelonia mydas)*
This is perhaps the best known of all the sea-going turtles, for it is the main ingredient of turtle soup. Its habitats range from the Barrier Reef of Australia to the Caribbean Islands. As its name suggests, the carapace is a uniform greenish-brown superimposed with darker brown and yellow markings. A fully grown specimen is about 3 ft. and may weigh up to 300 lb. The Green Turtle is a vegetable-eating creature, although it may take shellfish from time to time. To be kept successfully in captivity it needs plenty of salt water in which to live and ample space for swimming.

Loggerhead Turtle *(Caretta c. caretta)*
There are two main species of Loggerhead Turtle, the Atlantic and Pacific Loggerheads. The Loggerhead is much larger than the Green Turtle and can reach a length of 4 ft. The carapace is a rich reddish-brown and by contrast the plastron is completely yellow. The species gets its name from its unusually large head, which is very wide compared to its length. The Atlantic species was once plentiful but is now on the decline, due mainly to the fact that the beaches where it once lived have become commercialized and the females have been frightened away. Newly hatched Loggerheads have been known to mistake the bright lights of beach huts for the sea and many have been killed on the coastal highways. The Loggerhead is by nature carnivorous and feeds on jellyfish, crabs, and small fish. The Pacific species is still maintaining constant numbers, thanks mainly to the Australian Government who have banned building on certain beaches where the Loggerhead is known to breed. The Loggerhead is seldom used to make turtle soup, but its eggs are still taken as a delicacy.

Hawksbill Turtle *(Eretmochelys imbricata)*
Smaller in size than its cousins, the Hawksbill has the same geographical territory. The other name of this colourful creature is the Tortoiseshell Turtle, as this is the species from which tortoiseshell is extracted. The carapace when clean has radiating lines of yellow, red, and black on a light-brown ground colour. As in the Loggerhead, the plastron is yellow. Vegetarian by nature, the Hawksbill starts life as a carnivore but by the time it is one year old has turned to feeding on seaweed and the algae that grows along the shores.

Loggerhead Turtle   *Caretta c. caretta*

The poor creature has been hunted for its flesh, eggs, and shell, and was persecuted so much in the Fiji Islands that it became very scarce in this region. This species is now legally protected, and during the breeding season from November to February it is an offence even to collect its eggs.

Leathery Turtle *(Dermochelys coriacea)*, also called **Leatherback Turtle, Luth** or **Trunk Turtle**

The largest of all living turtles, the Leathery or Leatherback Turtle cannot possibly be confused with any other. A length of 6 ft. is not uncommon and some specimens reach 8 ft. As its name suggests, the Leatherback has a soft pliable carapace similar to wet leather. It has no commercial value although the eggs are occasionally taken. The carapace is completely black with five ridges running the full length. The head and limbs are a uniform black with a pale pink underside. This turtle, too, was in danger of complete extinction but is now completely protected in its entire geographical range, which incidentally is not as far reaching as that of the previously mentioned species. The Leatherback feeds mainly on jellyfish but will take crabs, fish, and other marine life.

Red Eared Terrapin *(Pseudemys scripta elegans)*, also called **Mobile Terrapin**

Subspecies of this turtle or terrapin are found in all the southern states of North America. All the subspecies are very closely linked and will readily interbreed. The Red Eared species is the most common and is sold in pet stores throughout the world. Business has been so brisk in recent years that special farms have been set up to breed the creature for export. The carapace is green in colour with fine yellow reticulations on each carapace plate. As the turtle grows the green ground colour becomes much less marked and in extreme old age may even turn black. The plastron is a vivid yellow and in young specimens has horseshoe-shaped blotches on each plastron plate. The head and limbs are also green in colour and fine yellow lines run the full length of each limb and of the head and neck. There is a red patch behind each eye. The species is also known as the Red Eared Slider, owing to the way it slides into the water whenever approached. It is an aquatic turtle and only comes on land to breed or to bask in the sun.

The male is much smaller than the female and was at one time thought to be a completely different species. It is possible to distinguish male from female by looking at the nails of the forefeet,

Leathery Turtle   *Dermochelys coriacea*

Red-eared Terrapin *Pseudemys scripta elegans*

Eastern Painted Terrapin   *Chrysemys picta picta*

which in the male are longer than the hind ones, while in the female the nails are the same length, both hind and fore.

The Red Eared Terrapin is unbelievably prolific; collectors have been known to dig up 3,000 eggs in the course of one afternoon. The female lays two or three clutches of eggs from April to July with as many as twenty eggs in each clutch. Newly hatched terrapins are approximately 1 in. long, and they are prayed upon by racoons, skunks, snakes, dogs, and cats, so it is not surprising that many never reach maturity. Man himself takes more than his fair share for pets and fish bait.

Yellow Bellied Terrapin *(Pseudemys scripta scripta)*
This species is very closely related to the Red Eared Slider and inhabits the south-eastern states of America. It is not unlike the Red Eared species in colour and carapace markings, and the two species interbreed. The carapace is a uniform green marked with yellow, while the plastron is all yellow and sometimes marked on the forepart. The distinguishing feature of the species is a yellow mark that appears on both sides of the terrapin's head.

Painted Terrapin *(Chrysemys picta)*
Although newly hatched terrapins of this species are very often confused with those of the Yellow Bellied Terrapin, the adults are easily distinguishable. The carapace of the Painted Terrapin is quite flat and a drab brownish-green in colour. The head and legs are striped with green and yellow and sometimes red. The largely unmarked plastron is pale yellow although some subspecies may have a ventral marking. One type or another of this species will be found in all parts of the United States. The known subspecies include Eastern Painted *(Chrysemys picta picta)*, Midland Painted *(Chrysemys picta marginata)*, Southern Painted *(Chrysemys picta dorsalis)*, and Western Painted *(Chrysemys picta bellis)*. A fully grown specimen may reach 9 in. in length. Newly hatched terrapins of the Southern species are easily identified by a yellow dorsal line, which runs the full length of the carapace.

Diamondback Terrapin *(Malaclemys terrapin terrapin)*
The Diamondback is perhaps one of the largest species of terrapin to inhabit the United States. The slate-grey carapace is ornamented with intricate lines of black and white, accompanied by lines of red along the outer edges of the plastron. The spotted head has red markings along the jaw bones giving the impression of red lips. The

Southern Painted Terrapin   *Chrysemys picta dorsalis*

Diamondback prefers brackish waters and if kept in fresh water for any length of time will develop fungus infections on the carapace. It lives in river estuaries, especially those on the Atlantic coast. This species of turtle is considered a great delicacy and is bred on special farms for this purpose.

Mississippi Map Terrapin *(Graptemys kohni)*
As its name suggests, the Mississippi Map Terrapin inhabits the warmer climes of the Mississippi valley south of the Missouri River. The carapace varies in colour from sandy-brown to dark grey, and is ridged along the dorsal line of the high-peaked shell. The rear marginals are serrated and the plastron is densely patterned. There are striking yellow stripes on the legs and behind each eye. In captivity the Mississippi Map Terrapin requires warmer quarters than the other American species.

Another species of Map Terrapin found in the central southern United States, the False Map Terrapin *(Graptemys pseudographica)* is very closely related to the Mississippi species but lacks the yellow eye stripe.

Common Snapping Terrapin *(Chelydra s. serpentinia)*
This is a very ferocious species, and when surprised or frightened, instead of taking cover as other turtles would, the Snapper stands its ground and snaps at anything that moves. Its speed of attack is incredible in view of its rather cumbersome body. The powerful, heavy jaws can inflict some quite horrific wounds. The other outstanding feature of this species is its long trailing tail. The oval-shaped carapace is dark greyish-brown in colour, as is the rest of the body. Projections on each side of the body connect the carapace to the poorly developed plastron. The Snapper's diet consists of 75 per cent vegetable matter and 25 per cent animal matter such as crayfish, snails, and carrion. Specimens are kept as pets and apparently have a very agreeable disposition when tamed. The species is a native of the United States.

Alligator Snapping Terrapin *(Macrochelys temmincki)*
This species is much larger than the Common species; weights have been recorded of nearly 250 lbs, but much smaller specimens than this have enough strength to pull a man's weight with ease. This species is also a native of the United States. The hard-shelled eggs of the Alligator Snapper are not unlike table tennis balls. Unlike the Common Snapper the diet of the Alligator Snapper

Mississippi Map Terrapin   *Graptemys kohni*

Common Snapping Terrapin   *Chelydra s. serpentinia*

consists mainly of fish. To catch its prey the Alligator Snapper lies at the bottom of a pool with its jaws open. Inside the mouth there is a worm-like projection that wriggles about to attract passing fish into the turtle's jaws, which then snap shut. This species is rarely available in pet stores.

Musk *(Sternoth Aerus)* Mud *(Kinosternon)* Terrapins

There are many subspecies of both these types of terrapin. They inhabit most streams and pools from the Atlantic coast of the United States to the Mexican border. The carapace is oval in shape and slightly keeled, and smaller than that of Red Eared Terrapin. The main colour is brown and sometimes looks almost black. The markings vary considerably from white and black spots to plain, unmarked carapaces, although most species have lightly striped heads and limbs. Musk and Mud Turtles are very unpopular as pets, as when frightened they omit a very unpleasant, pungent odour, which is difficult to eradicate.

Yellow Spotted Sideneck *(Podocnemis unifilis)* and Orange Spotted Sideneck *(Podocnemis expansa)*

Both these species inhabit the tropical jungles of the Amazon. They are shy, secretive creatures and are rarely seen in pet stores. Their name comes from a side action of the neck. The carapace, plastron, head, and limbs are entirely grey, the only distinguishing marks being yellow head spots in the *Unifilis* species and orange head spots in *Expansa.* Although legally protected, Sidenecks are hunted for food by native Indians.

Bog Terrapin *(Clemmys muhlenbergi)*

This rare turtle is only found in certain swampy areas in the United States. Measures are being taken to protect the species wherever possible. The carapace is dark brown and there are red or yellow markings on the larger plates and also on each side of the head. Adult specimens rarely reach a length of 4 in.

Cooter Terrapin *(Pseudemys conicinna)*

This species is very similar to the Painted Turtle, and inhabits the same regions. The Cooter has a dark-brown carapace, which is unmarked except at the edges of the marginal plates, which are tinged with red and orange. There are small yellow stripes on each side of the head. The Cooter is often available in pet stores.

Chicken Terrapin *(Deirochelys reticularia)*
This species is found extensively in the southern United States and was at one time sold in fish markets for food. It is commonly sold as a pet. The brownish-black carapace is unmarked but the plastron is a vivid bright yellow. For its full adult size of about 6 in., the legs and head are very short.

Spotted Terrapin *(Clemmys guttata)*
This species comes from the colder climates of the eastern parts of the United States, and is one of the more hardy species. The dark-blue carapace is covered with a profusion of yellow marks, and whilst some specimens may have just a few of these spots, others may be entirely covered with them. The head and limbs are similarly marked. Specimens kept in captivity should be provided with plenty of space in which they can wander at will, as well as plenty of water.

Malayan Pond Terrapin *(Malayemis subtrijuga)*
This is a very delicate species and needs a lot of attention when kept in captivity. Snails, whole unshelled shrimps, and fresh meat must form the main part of the diet if specimens are to survive. The dark-brown carapace is sharply ridged along its entire length, especially on the vertebrals. The marginals are edged with yellow and so is the head. Specimens reach only 4 in. when adult.

Florida Soft Shell *(Trionyx ferox)*, **Common Soft Shell** *(Trionyx muticus)* and **Ganges Soft Shell** *(Trionyx gangeticus)*
These three main species of Soft Shell Terrapin have very similar shape and colour characteristics. The carapace, as the name of the species suggests, is soft and leathery to the touch and completely round in shape, and hence totally adapted to the terrapin's habit of lying motionless on the muddy river bed. The drab olive-brown colour also helps to camouflage the terrapin as it lies in wait for its prey of fish. The Ganges Turtle has reticulated dark lines all over the plastron. All Soft Shelled Terrapins have long necks and a protruding snout. They are wholly aquatic and come ashore solely to sunbathe and breed, and then only when the weather is favourable.

Spotted Terrapin   *Clemmys guttata*

Florida Soft Shell   *Trionyx ferox*

Matamata Terrapin *Chelys fimbriata*

Matamata Terrapin *(Chelys fimbriata)*

The chapter would be incomplete without a description of the strange and wonderful Matamata. The dark-brown, horny carapace is covered with a series of wart-like plates, which gives this species its ugly appearance. It inhabits the tropical rivers and streams of South America, especially those in Brazil and Peru, and the Amazon River. It is a side-necked terrapin and the very long neck is curled under the edge of the marginal plates for protection. The head is very small and the protruding eyes are very near the snout. Like the Soft Shell Terrapins, the Matamata lies in wait for its prey, and has a unique way of catching its food. Fringe-like pieces of skin on the neck are waved to attract the attention of the fish. As soon as a fish comes near enough, the Matamata opens its mouth and sucks fish and water into its throat. Specimens rarely become available but they can be seen in zoos and museums throughout the world.

Housing and feeding turtles

The majority of turtles sold as pets are young and possibly newly hatched. The most common species available in pet stores are the American species Red Eared Sliders and Painted and Map Terrapins. Other more exotic types do appear occasionally on breeders' lists but they are much more expensive and harder to maintain in perfect health. When selecting a terrapin for a pet, choose one that tries to swim when held clear of the water. Other points to look for are the same as those given for tortoises.

Unfortunately at least 75 per cent of all terrapins sold as pets live only a few weeks, because the new owner is almost always innocently ignorant of the three basic needs of terrapins: heat, light, and the correct diet. When provided with these three basic needs the terrapin makes an interesting and easily kept pet.

The first requirement is of course somewhere to house the terrapin. Newly hatched terrapins are approximately 2 in. in diameter but grow at an alarming rate in their first six months of life, and must be given plenty of space if they are not to become overcrowded. Without doubt the best way of housing terrapins is in an aquarium, and the larger the aquarium the better. Aquariums can be expensive, especially the modern type with a plastic-covered frame and silicone-bonded glass, but the dearer type will be robust and stand much more wear and tear. An aquarium measuring 12 in. × 12 in. × 15 in. will comfortably house one terrapin, and one measuring 36 in. × 12 in. × 15 in. will accommodate three specimens.

All terrapins adore sunbathing, and somewhere for them to dry out completely must be provided, for example, a smooth rock protruding above the water line or a piece of cork on to which the terrapin can climb. Other aquarium furnishings can be added for decoration but will be of no practical use. The depth of water should be at least twice the terrapins' length from head to tail. Fresh, clean water is essential for good health. Any rocks or stones for the aquarium must be spotlessly clean with no protruding sharp edges, which may cut the terrapin's plastron as it climbs out of the water.

The terrapin must be kept warm at all times or it will not feed. The water should be warmed with an aquarium water heater of the type used for tropical fish; the most efficient type incorporates a thermostat and neon indicator, and this makes it unnecessary to switch off the heater when the temperature reaches the required level. Terrapins do well at temperatures between 29°C and 34°C. Below this level they may stop feeding and may even go into hibernation. Excessive temperatures are just as harmful as they may cause dehydration of the terrapin's body tissue. The aquarium should be heated night and day as fluctuations of temperature may also cause feeding problems. Light for artificial sunbathing can be provided by an ordinary electric lamp of about 60–100 watts. Fluorescent light should not be used as it does not give off the required amount of heat for sunbathing. The light should be switched on in the morning and left on for a minimum of eight hours; it should not be left on all night as this will give rise to excessive temperatures, and terrapins fare better if they are left in darkness during the night. The rock on which the terrapins sunbathe should be placed directly underneath the light.

The aquarium should be cleaned as often as possible, and this task is much easier if an aquarium hand pump is used. A pump consists of two lengths of hose connected in the middle by a rubber suction ball.

For the young terrapin's carapace and plastron to grow at its fullest rate calcium must be provided and this is best given in the food. Some people recommend submerging plaster of paris in the aquarium to provide calcium, but the alkali may possibly harm the terrapin's eyes. Terrapins must have a properly controlled, balanced diet. Food dirties the aquarium water so it is best to feed the terrapin in a separate bowl of water that can be easily cleaned. Food can only be eaten in water and so the water in the bowl must be deep enough to allow the terrapin to submerge its head and body. The temperature of the water in the feeding bowl should be the same as in the aquarium, otherwise the terrapin may not feed. Pet stores sell a dried insect food especially prepared for turtles, and this can be fed once a week as a roughage supplement to the main diet, but although it contains a certain amount of calcium and protein it is insufficient on its own to sustain a growing terrapin. The proper diet should include fish, fresh meat, green leaves of lettuce, and a small amount of fruit. Cuttlefish bone is by far the easiest source of calcium and this should be ground and sprinkled on all the food before it is offered. Cod-liver oil and orange juice also supply the vitamins and minerals required by terrapins. Tinned tuna fish and sardines are a convenient form of fish for turtles. The contents of the tin should be washed to remove all traces of oil and sauce, then sprinkled with cuttlefish bone and undiluted orange juice. The prepared fish can be kept in the freezer department of a refrigerator

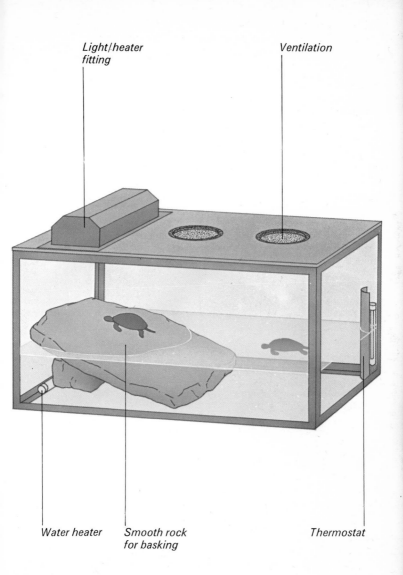

Light/heater fitting

Ventilation

Water heater

Smooth rock for basking

Thermostat

An aquarium suitable for terrapins

Terrapins should be fed in a separate bowl to avoid polluting the aquarium.

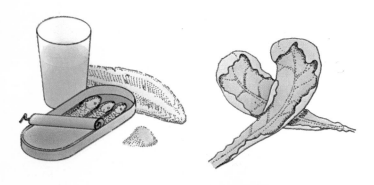

Sardines sprinkled with cuttlefish bone and orange juice, lettuce leaves, liver, chicken, entrails, and earthworms make up a balanced diet for terrapins.

until needed. Meat can consist of liver, beef, chicken, entrails, and earthworms; on no account should fatty foods be offered as these will cause the terrapin to choke if they solidify in the throat. The best time for feeding terrapins is in the early evening when the temperatures are at their highest.

Index

Distributors for
Bartholomew Pet Books

Australia

Book Trade : Tudor Distributors Pty. Limited, 14 Mars Road,
Lane Cove 2066, New South Wales, Australia

Canada

Pet Trade : Burgham Sales Ltd., 558 McNicoll Avenue,
Willowdale (Toronto), Ontario, Canada M2H 2E1
Book Trade : Clarke Irwin and Company, Limited,
791 St. Clair Avenue W., Toronto, Canada M6C 1B8

New Zealand

Pet Trade : Masterpet Products Limited,
7 Kaiwharawhara Road, Wellington, New Zealand
Book Trade : Whitcoulls Limited, Trade Department, Private Bag,
Auckland, Wellington, or Christchurch, New Zealand

South Africa

Book Trade : McGraw-Hill Book Company (S.A.) (Pty.) Limited,
P.O. Box 23423, Joubert Park, Johannesburg,
South Africa

U.S.A.

Pet Trade : Pet Supply Imports Inc., P.O. Box 497, Chicago,
Illinois, U.S.A.
Book Trade : The Two Continents Publishing Group Limited,
30 East 42nd Street, New York, N.Y. 10017, U.S.A.